A Dilbert Book
by Scott Adams

Andrews and McMeel
A Universal Press Syndicate Company
Kansas City

For Pam, my role model

Introduction

You may think this book is simply a cynical way to cash in on the popularity of the strip without doing much of anything in the way of extra work. And you'd be largely correct about that. But look at it this way: After you enjoy it, you can give it to somebody else as a gift. That's something you can't do with, say, a bottle of wine (at least not gracefully). A Dilbert book is a rare opportunity to satisfy your greed and your nagging gift-giving guilt at the same time. It's a win-win scenario.

The only problem is that the book doesn't quite lay flat after you've pawed your way through it. You'll need an alibi.

I recommend that you get a felt-tipped pen and write "Best Wishes—Scott Adams" on the inside cover and try to pass it off as an autographed copy. You could even sketch a little Dogbert in there. If he looks a little deformed, just say my arm was in a sling.*

If the recipient hunts me down to verify your clam, I'll lie for you. You have my word on that.

On a related topic, many of you have written to ask how you can join a Dilbert/Dogbert fan club, mailing list, cult, or paramilitary force. So far, all we have is a mailing list. There are two benefits to being on the mailing list: 1.) You get a free Dilbert newsletter if we feel like it, and 2.) When Dogbert conquers the world, you will form a new ruling class.

To get on the mailing list, write:

E-mail: scottadams@aol.com

Snail Mail: Dilbert Mailing List
              United Media
              200 Park Avenue
              New York, NY 10166

Scott Adams

*If if looks better than I draw it, I hate you.

32

41

44

50

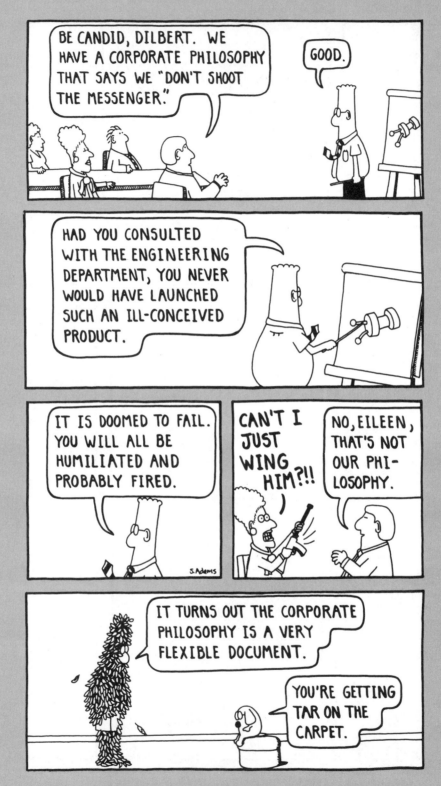

65

Panel 1: DID YOU HEAR THAT THE TINY EAST EUROPEAN COUNTRY OF ELBONIA HAS ABANDONED COMMUNISM? / WHOA! BIG CHANGES AHEAD.

Panel 2: ELBONIA: MONDAY / MUD FARM

Panel 3: ELBONIA: TUESDAY / MY TREE / MY MUD FARM / MY PIG / MY FEET

Panel 4: DILBERT, I'M SENDING YOU TO ELBONIA TO OPEN OUR NEW SUB-SIDIARY. / ELBONIA?

Panel 5: BUT THEY ONLY RENOUNCED COMMUNISM LAST WEEK!! THEY DON'T UNDERSTAND CAPITALISM OR ECONOMICS. THEY HAVE NO APPRECIATION OF THE REAL WORLD.

Panel 6: ...HE THINKS THEY'LL MAKE FINE ENGINEERS.

Panel 7: DILBERT ARRIVES AT THE EX-COMMUNIST COUNTRY OF ELBONIA. / I NEED A FLIGHT TO YOUR CAPITAL.

Panel 8: FOR A MOMENT I WAS WORRIED THAT THIS BACKWARD LITTLE COUNTRY WOULDN'T HAVE A COMMUTER FLIGHT.

Panel 9: I HATE LIVING NEAR THE AIRPORT.

HERE'S A "HELP WANTED" AD FOR A BABYSITTER.

I COULD DO THAT. KIDS LOVE DINOSAURS.

ONE PROBLEM.

YOUR SPECIES IS KNOWN TO BE CARNIVOROUS.

I'LL PUT "STRICT DISCIPLINARIAN" ON MY RESUME.

HI. I'M BOB. I CALLED EARLIER ABOUT THE BABY-SITTING JOB.

TO BE HONEST, WE DIDN'T KNOW YOU WERE A DINOSAUR WHEN YOU CALLED...

THAT'S OKAY. I DIDN'T KNOW YOU WERE YUPPIE BIGOTS.

...WE SHOULD AT LEAST INTERVIEW HIM. NOBODY ELSE EVEN ANSWERED OUR AD FOR A BABYSITTER.

FRANKLY, BOB, WE'RE CONCERNED THAT YOU MIGHT TRY TO EAT THE CHILDREN.

WELL, OF COURSE, IN THAT CASE THERE WOULD BE NO CHARGE FOR THE EVENING.

HE'S MORE THAN FAIR.